Weathering
The
Storms

Weathering The Storms

Jim Wood

Books by Jim and Susan Wood:
Every Child Deserves Straight A's
A place to call HOME
When Two Become One
Weathering the Storms
The Life of PRAYER series:
    Calling Him Daddy
    Hearing His Voice
    Embracing His Will
Video series, *A Place to Call Home*:
Important Issues Concerning You and Your Family

For retreats on marriage, parenting, prayer, etc.
Contact:
Jim Wood Ministries
P.O. Box 1600
Pigeon Forge, TN 37868
865/429-4300
JWood@wvr.org

Wears Valley Ranch newsletters:
Wears Valley Ranch
3601 Lyon Springs Road
Sevierville, TN 37862
865/429-5437
www.WVR.org

LOC: 00-91779
ISBN: 0-9701855-1-0
Cover Photography © 2000 by Morris Press

Printed in the United States by Morris Publishing
3212 East Highway 30 • Kearney, NE 68847 • 1800-650-7888

Dedicated to Paul

I will always be grateful to God for the privilege of being your father. Your suffering has taught me more than any school. Your courage has strengthened mine. Your compassion for the weak and your joy in the midst of pain have been a witness to the grace of our Lord. I'm glad you are my son. I'm even more grateful to call you my brother in Christ. I love you and thank God continually for you!

CONTENTS

Therefore, everyone who hears these words of mine and puts them into practice is like a wise man who built his house on the rock. The rain came down, the streams rose, and the winds blew and beat against that house, yet it did not fall, because it had its foundation on the rock. But everyone who hears these words of mine and does not put them into practice is like a foolish man who built his house on sand. The rain came down, the streams rose, and the winds blew and beat against that house, and it fell with a great crash.

Matthew 7:24-27.

Storm Warning

MANY PEOPLE GET MARRIED anticipating that everything will go well, only to be terribly disappointed to discover that life is hard. The reason we take vows when we get married is because of the hard parts. *We promise to stay together* for better or *for worse*, for richer or *for poorer*, *in sickness* and in health, *'til death do us part*. Then, we act as if none of the negative things will ever happen to us. For us it will always be *for better, for richer, and in health.* But, life has a way of bringing the unexpected, and difficult and painful things begin to happen. We plan wonderful things for our future. Of course, we're going to have children, and they're going to come along at the right time, but somehow, things don't go as planned.

I knew a couple who got married and had a baby nine months and two days after the wedding. This wasn't their plan. While children are a gift from the Lord, it's nice to have a little time to get to know each other first. You may be one of the twenty percent of couples who experiences infertility and can't have children. If you want to have children, this is a brutal storm.

There are also those of us who are blessed to have children right when we planned it, but the child born to us wasn't what we had imagined. Our first child was born with Spina Bifida and has had over twenty surgeries. Many people are not prepared for the unexpected stress chronic medical problems bring to their relationship. Over eighty percent of couples who have a child with a serious birth defect divorce. They decide, "I can't handle this. This isn't what I signed up for."

This is what we signed up for! We said for better or for worse, for richer or for poorer, *in sickness* and in health, *'til death do us part.*

Over and over, as I counsel various couples about the difficulties in their marriage and family life, it becomes evident that the reason they're in chaos is not just because storms came, but because storms came and exposed the fact that they had not been doing what God says to do. When the storms hit, you find out what your house is made of.

We live in the mountains of east Tennessee and we get some high winds. When these storms come, we are grateful for the two by six construction used to build our home instead of the usual two by four frame. We appreciate the builder and his level of competence. We thank God for the designer and his blueprints.

We've lived in New England and in the Deep South. We've never been so hot as we were on a steamy July day in New England, and we've never been so cold as during an ice storm in the Deep South. Why? The houses in New England were built to withstand snowstorms, and because it is seldom hot, very few houses are air-conditioned. In the Deep South, houses are constructed to handle heat, but the heating systems for the usually mild winters are not built to handle blizzard conditions or ice storms. People build houses based on the environment. When the storms come, what you have been building is exposed, for better or for worse.

During the storms, areas where we have not been obedient to the Lord are exposed in our lives. Those areas of vulnerability and weakness, in which we have not been doing what God says to do, suddenly become apparent. The irony, however, is that when these areas get exposed, most of us try to solve the problem by doing something else that is disobedient to God. The excuse becomes, "I have to do this now, because I have a real problem now, and this is the best solution." Never mind the fact that the plan involves further disobedience to God's word. People often patch up their houses that way, too. But when the next storm hits, the house isn't just damaged. Because of its patched and weakened condition, it is destroyed.

My question is, "If you got into the mess you're in by not doing what God says, why would you try to improve your situation by disobeying what God says again?" If you truly know God, the only rational course is to obey him.

If the builder who built your house needed to follow the designer's plan, how much more important is it for us to obey the Creator of marriage and the family when he gives us his plan? When you build, you don't just round up building materials and start hammering. You study the blueprint. In the case of your marriage, not only is there a plan, the architect is God. God invented marriage and family. We didn't begin as animals in the Garden of Eden discovering each other, noticing similarities, and deciding to pool talents. Instead, God designed man and woman for each other and planned marriage to be a picture of the relationship between Christ and the church.

The reason so many marriages aren't joyful and fulfilling is because people aren't following the God-ordained plan. If you don't follow the plan, the parts don't fit. It just doesn't work. But, this is not the fault of the designer. The builder must carefully follow the blueprint.

Oftentimes in marriage, things fall apart and end prematurely because people don't know their roles. They've never learned what God says about the plan we're supposed to follow. If we're going to do it God's way, we have to study and learn God's way. There is a plan!

Every life, every marriage will be challenged by storms. Jesus says the difference between the house that stands and the house that falls is the foundation. Guess what? The foundation is foundational! While this is obvious, how many people do you know who live their lives as if it were not so? Many people are totally consumed with external appearances and end up building on shifting sand. They never dig down to establish the things that are most important.

As I have supervised the construction of various buildings, I have been repeatedly disappointed to see how much of the cost goes into places people will never see. A huge chunk of the budget is spent before the aesthetic beauty is begun. Lots of dirt has to be moved, trenches dug, pipe laid, concrete poured, and other unglamorous labors accomplished before the project becomes exciting and satisfying.

We must go down to the rock and put in steel and concrete to make the building solid, because we want it to last. So much effort is required for things that nobody will ever see, so that what people do see will remain rock-solid. It can't be shaken when the storms of life come. It's built to withstand storms; therefore, it's worth the investment.

It's pretty sad to watch news footage of multi-million dollar mansions in California sliding down the hills. It's absolutely amazing to watch somebody's three million dollar home washing into the ocean. What was it anchored to? They apparently anchored it to dirt, not rock. They didn't go down to a solid foundation. They built on that spot even though no solid ground was available. It was such a beautiful view – *this year!*

The same thing has happened on Cape Cod. Generations back people built their main dwellings inland and put little shanties on the beach. They called them camps. Even wealthy people built only rustic shanties on the beach. The reason was because they knew that eventually a big enough storm would come and wash their beach house away. By the nineteen eighties, young urban professionals were making fortunes and building huge homes on the Cape Cod beaches. Now, when the storms come and take these mansions away, the federal government steps in to pay to rebuild. Wealthy people feel free to build mansions, because they have federal insurance money with which to gamble.

It's not really a gamble, however. It's a sure thing that storms are coming. Yet, our tax dollars are used to rebuild on the same site where disaster is guaranteed. For two thousand years, it has been a well-known fact that if you build on the sand, the storms will take your house away.

In our culture, we are not only building on sand with costly construction materials; we are also building on sand with our lives, our marriages, and our families.

Build on Rock

Therefore, everyone who hears these words of mine and puts them into practice is like a wise man who built his house on the rock. The rain came down, the streams rose, and the winds blew and beat against that house; yet, it did not fall, because it had its foundation on the rock.[1]

We need to build on rock, and we must choose the high ground. Don't go inviting trouble. Understand that there are certain areas where it is not smart to build. There are certain things in your life that you know don't belong. Choose the high ground! Choose the areas that are less vulnerable to storms and the floods that follow.

If you have a problem with alcohol, don't hang out in bars. If you have a problem with a wandering eye, don't buy magazines or view videos that feed the lust. Choose your friends carefully. Be careful who you have business lunches with and under what circumstances. Sin is waiting at the door. Be honest with yourself about your vulnerabilities.

The person who is most susceptible to sin is the person who denies that it could happen to him. I don't want to do anything to give anybody, especially my wife, any reason to even wonder if there might be a problem. I want to make deposits in our trust account. I want to build trust into my most important relationship. I don't want to make withdrawals. Change your line of work, if necessary, to protect your marriage. If you want to make your marriage work, you can make the necessary adjustments.

It's better to lose your business than to lose your soul. Jesus says it isn't just the one who hears his word that is building on the rock, but the one who hears his word and puts it into practice.

Building on the rock always involves obedience to God's word.

You will never get out of a mess by disobedience; you'll just get into another mess. If you refuse to follow God's principles, you will absolutely make matters worse.

If you want to build your marriage on the rock, it begins with obedience to God's word. This is where you start. The storms will come and if you have built in obedience, you will weather any storm. God is the one who will see you through. God has already committed himself to seeing you through. God always keeps his promises.

Susan and I have seen God keep his promises in our lives through all kinds of storms. Sometimes, our obedience has looked like insanity to other people, but we had to decide to obey God anyway. He is the only one we can always trust to see us through. Other people may not be around when the storms come. God will always be there for us.

Being obedient to God is not a formula to prevent us from going through hard times. We will all go through hard times, whether we are obedient or not. But when we are obedient, we have God's promises to see us through. God allows us to have rainy days, not only because rain makes the plants grow, but also because it sure is nice when the sun comes out after the rain. God also lets us have periods of drought so that we will appreciate the rainy days. God knows what we need, and he has promised that if we will do what he says, he will see us through.

MATERIALS MAKE A MAJOR DIFFERENCE,

and we're not talking material things. In I Corinthians 3:10-15 we read:

> By the grace God has given me, I laid a foundation as an expert builder, and someone else is building on it. But each one should be careful how he builds. For no one can lay any foundation other than the one already laid, which is Jesus Christ.
>
> If any man builds on this foundation using gold, silver, costly stones, wood, hay or straw, his work will be shown for what it is, because the Day will bring it to light. It will be revealed with fire, and the fire will test the quality of each man's work. If what he has built survives, he will receive his reward. If it is burned up, he will suffer loss; he himself will be saved, but only as one escaping through the flames.

The apostle Paul reminds us that whether we build using gold, silver, costly stones, wood, hay or straw, our work will be shown for what it is "because the day will bring it to light. It will be revealed with fire and the fire will test the quality of each person's work."

What is he talking about? Is he suggesting that if you want to do well in the day of difficulty you need to amass gold, silver and costly stones? Jesus says that you are a very foolish person if you try to amass things that will perish. We know that wood, hay and straw perish rapidly in a fire or a storm. But, we assume that gold, silver and costly stones will survive. Actually, all of these things will perish.

"Do not lay up for yourselves treasures on earth where moth and rust corrupt and where thieves break in and steal." What do moths eat? Clothes and fabrics that are not in use. What about rust? Metal is most prone to rust when it is not being used. The expression, "I'd rather burn out than rust out" speaks of a desire to be put to use. What do thieves break in and steal? Thieves break in and steal luxuries. When was the last time you heard of a thief stealing sheets, blankets, or groceries? Thieves are after the high-ticket items. They steal the stuff we didn't really need to begin with, generally the gold, silver and precious stones.

If we invest our lives in stuff we don't need, instead of investing our lives in meeting the needs of others, we are setting ourselves up for disaster. So, what materials make the difference? We need to build a home that is constructed with honesty, faith, affection, diligence, honor, and the other virtues that grow out of a heart yielded to God.

Susan was diligent to invest time every night at bedtime with our kids. I had devotions with them when I was at home, but whether I was home or not, Susan made sure they had time with their parents. This investment, which was costly, has paid off with huge dividends. Our boys have confided in us, even through the high school and college years. When my boys see me, they still give me a hug and a kiss. And, these are manly guys. But, they are absolutely relaxed and secure in their affection for their dad, and, of course, for their mom.

What are you building in your relationships right now? Are you spending the time required to show your spouse, "I love you more than I love my job, and even more than I love myself?" Most of us convey to our mate in hundreds of ways, "After me darling, you are number one." This is a sad truth. We need to examine our hearts and behave in a way that communicates honestly: "I want you to know that after Jesus, you're number one. I put your interests ahead of my own."

One of the main ways a married person shows love for Jesus is in showing love for their spouse. Do you want to do something Jesus will really appreciate? Be good to your spouse. Treat them right. Show them you would rather meet their needs than yours. If you will work on this, when the storms hit, your home will stand firm, because there's a foundation. You've been doing what God says.

Surviving Your Worst Nightmare

I GET PHONE CALLS from people in all kinds of crisis situations. Not long ago, I got a phone call from a girl who said, "I need help. I am a thirteen-year-old caught in the middle of a very dysfunctional family."

I thought to myself, "You're a precocious thirteen-year-old who has learned some powerful lingo." As we talked, I learned she was right about her very dysfunctional family. Unfortunately, this family, with all their problems, is typical of many.

A person called to discuss whether or not to file for a legal separation or seek guardianship of an alcoholic spouse. This person wanted to protect the spouse and the rest of the family from the dangerous behavior of the inebriated spouse, especially driving while under the influence. The person said to me, "This is my worst nightmare!"

It reminded me of something Job said after being hit with a barrage of disasters: "What I feared has come upon me; what I dreaded has happened to me."[2] All of us have been through storms, and at times, we wonder if God isn't preparing us for more storms to come. Most of us have a worst-case scenario in our minds, and we're hoping and praying it's not going to happen.

Many years ago, a woman spoke at the famous Intervarsity Missions Conference at Urbana, Illinois. She was speaking to thousands of university students. She said, "When I was growing up, I was afraid to yield my life to Jesus Christ, because I thought if I did I would end up as an old maid missionary to Africa. After years of struggling, I finally surrendered to the Lord, and now, I'm an old maid missionary to Africa." Then she said, "You know, I wouldn't have it any other way. I found out that the thing I feared is actually wonderful. One great benefit is that God has shown me that he is all I need."

Sometimes God whispers quietly to our spirits to prepare us for a storm that will test our faith and try us and cause us, if we're wise, to run to him and take refuge. He warns us because he loves us and doesn't want us to be destroyed.

EVEN PEOPLE who don't know the Bible well know the story of Job. Most people have identified with Job at certain points in life. What we sometimes fail to remember, however, is that Job didn't have access to the book of Job. He was a man with an idyllic life. When sudden misery came upon him, he had questions. As he suffered, he developed an even deeper abiding faith in God.

One day when Job's sons and daughters were feasting and drinking wine at the oldest brother's house, a messenger came to Job and said, 'The oxen were plowing and the donkeys were grazing nearby, and the Sabeans attacked and carried them off. They put the servants to the sword, and I am the only one who has escaped to tell you!'

While he was still speaking, another messenger came and said, 'The fire of God fell from the sky and burned up the sheep and the servants, and I am the only one who has escaped to tell you!'

While he was still speaking, another messenger came and said, 'The Chaldeans formed three raiding parties and swept down on your camels and carried them off. They put the servants to the sword, and I am the only one who has escaped to tell you!'

While he was still speaking, yet another messenger came and said, 'Your sons and daughters were feasting and drinking wine at the oldest brother's house, when suddenly a mighty wind swept in from the desert and struck the four corners of the house. It collapsed on them and they are dead, and I am the only one who has escaped to tell you!'

At this, Job got up and tore his robe and shaved his head. Then he fell to the ground in worship and said: 'Naked I came from my mother's womb, and naked I will depart. The LORD gave and the LORD has taken away; may the name of the LORD be praised.'

In all this, Job did not sin by charging God with wrongdoing.[3]

The LORD said to Satan, 'Very well, then, he is in your hands; but you must spare his life.'

So, Satan went out from the presence of the LORD and afflicted Job with painful sores from the soles of his feet to the top of his head.

Then Job took a piece of broken pottery and scraped himself with it as he sat among the ashes.

His wife said to him, 'Are you still holding on to your integrity? Curse God and die!'

He replied, 'You are talking like a foolish woman. Shall we accept good from God, and not trouble?' In all this, Job did not sin in what he said.

When Job's three friends, Eliphaz the Temanite, Bildad the Shuhite and Zophar the Naamathite, heard about all the troubles that had come upon him, they set out from their homes and met together by agreement to go and sympathize with him and comfort him.

When they saw him from a distance, they could hardly recognize him; they began to weep aloud, and they tore their robes and sprinkled dust on their heads.

Then they sat on the ground with him for seven days and seven nights. No one said a word to him, because they saw how great his suffering was.[4]

'What I feared has come upon me; what I dreaded has happened to me.'[5]

SO MANY PEOPLE going through tragic difficulties say the same thing: "This is my worst nightmare." In the midst of a good life, Job said, "What I feared has come upon me; what I dreaded has happened to me." He had been greatly blessed, but he obviously had had a question in his mind, "What if it's not always like this? What if disaster strikes one day?"

Disaster did strike. Job came to the point where he was literally sitting among the ashes. Things that had been beautiful were now in ruins. Things that had brought joy and encouragement, reminding him daily that God loved him and had blessed him, were now taken from him. Job was sitting in misery, seeking to hold on to his faith.

I don't know what your worst nightmare is, that particular encounter with tragedy that would make you sympathize with Job. Everyone's story is different, but all through life, we all know pain. Sometimes when it seems things are going great, suddenly they can all go wrong.

There are times when our loved ones do things that create a worse grief than if they had died. It doesn't diminish the love we have for them, but it would have been easier to grieve the loss of physical life than to see them take a grievously evil path that tempts us to despair.

A young married woman, who had lost her mother after a long debilitating disease, spoke to me about the greater heartbreak of losing her dad in a very different way after her mother was gone. He hadn't died, but his changed behavior made her wonder about his salvation. She didn't seem to know this man who had been her spiritual adviser, as she now watched him rebel against God. The father she thought she had always known was no longer with her. A man she didn't want to know had emerged.

Some people deal with the pain of their nightmare by suppressing it or pretending it doesn't exist. Their response is summed up in the expression, "D'Nile ain't just a river!" This is, perhaps, what turned this young woman's father into a rebel. He wasn't willing to truly grieve the pain of his loss and turn to God for comfort. Instead, he sought comfort in actions that were in direct disobedience to God's word.

There are all kinds of situations where denial can lead to further tragedy. Others can see it coming, but the people it will most deeply impact ignore the dark and ominous clouds on the horizon moving their way.

A friend called me recently to ask advice. His neighbors' teenage daughter had just attempted suicide. A family member discovered her unconscious and unresponsive in her bedroom. After the Rescue Squad took her away in an ambulance, my friend's wife drove the girl's mother to the hospital. The father met them there. At three a.m. as his daughter remained on life-support, he came into the waiting room where my friend's wife had been praying for hours and said in a disgusted tone, "She is so self-serving, always looking for ways to get attention!" At that point, it was still questionable whether the girl would even live. This was not a plea for attention, where a person takes pills, and then calls for help. This was a carefully planned and nearly successful attempt to die.

My friend's wife was horrified as she drove the mother home and heard, "She can't miss the end of the term. This could affect her admission to a good college."

Within forty-eight hours, the girl's father, an influential physician, had his daughter transferred from ICU to his home. The mother told my friends, "She's fine now. She'll be back in school on Monday." The issues that had driven the girl to take her own life were being completely ignored. The suicide note, which she had left to be found after she was dead, specifically spoke of her despair over the pressures she felt at school. The parents only seemed concerned with avoiding humiliation. My friends were concerned that the girl would not survive with no counseling and no sympathy even from her own parents. These parents have other children as well who can clearly see that their very lives are not as important as preserving the image of a stable family.

I told my friend that there is nothing we can do to make other people take their responsibilities seriously. I suggested ways to gently guide these parents toward the truth. Despite the evidence that these parents would rather pretend the suicide attempt never happened, I suggested sending them notes saying such things as, "We are praying for you as you deal with the particularly painful difficulties ahead." But, beyond showing love to the various members of the family, there is little that my friends can do to help. If your child's attempted suicide doesn't get your attention, it is unlikely that you will be prepared for the storms that follow. What a difference is seen in those who are prepared.

EVEN AS THIS BOOK was being written, dear friends of ours lost their twenty-seven year old son in a car accident. A wonderful Christian and robust athlete, their only son was taken without warning. The response of this family to such painful news was an extraordinary testimony to God's grace. Sorrowful? Of course, but not the sort of grief as those who have no hope.[6]

Their preparation for this nightmare was evident to all. Not only did it make it possible for them to survive their worst nightmare with peace and grace, they provided strength and comfort, as well as eternal perspective to all who came in contact with them during this time. Their faith not only sustained them, but also deepened through this tragedy.

The young man's mother was the first to be informed of his death. She was called out of her morning Bible Study class to receive the news. With her usual beautiful smile, she responded, "You always assume it will be someone else's child, but God is in control. He knows what he's doing. I don't have to know." Because their son had evidenced this same trust in his life, they could face their grief with confidence in his eternal security.

This foundational trust which she and her husband exhibited was also reflected in their only surviving child. Upon hearing the news of her brother's tragic death, his married sister, who had been his best friend, immediately called her brother-in-law and challenged him to give his life to Christ. "I'm so glad it was my brother and not you. I know he's in heaven. Please, realize that you need to trust Christ now before it's too late."

HOW DO WE ORIENT our thinking properly so that when the storms come, whatever they may be, we're ready? On the one hand, this involves recognizing that *there is a Sovereign God*. The universe is not run by chance. Our lives are not ruled by a statistical toss of a coin, where sooner or later it will come up tails. God is working all things together for the good of those who love him. But, this doesn't mean that everything is going to be good when it comes our way. It doesn't mean life will be easy and fun and if we just have enough faith, we won't have to go through hard times.

God doesn't promise health and wealth to anyone. Jesus said, "Lo, I am with you always, even to the end of the age."[7] This is the promise. And while Jesus did come so that we could have life and have it to the full, sometimes having life to the full involves discovering that God's strength is made perfect in our weakness.[8]

People come to see me and tell me about health problems or other difficult things happening in their lives that I'm very sorry to hear. I've said to close friends when they've told me the doctor's dire prognosis, "You may not live long enough to die of your illness." The doctor may believe, "You only have about nine months." The fact is your doctor may not live nine months. On the other hand, you may live a lot longer than nine months.

I was teaching on this subject at a conference center in North Carolina, and a man shared his testimony with me. He and his wife had been involved in ministry for many years when she was diagnosed with a very serious cancer and given only a few months to live. Because their lives had impacted so many people, there were many who came to their home to express their sympathy and love and to say goodbye to her.

They kept a guest book for these friends to sign and seven years later when the Lord finally called her home, thirty-five of the friends who had come to tell her goodbye had preceded her in death. Only the Lord knows how much time we have left. Never presume that you have another day. And, never presume that you don't. God is in control.

You probably know other people whose situations were ruled hopeless, and yet they lived on and on. Often the doctors don't understand why. Life is uncertain, but God is trustworthy. Whatever difficulty we face, the goal is to face it holding on to the everlasting arms, knowing that he's holding on to us. Job experienced horrible things, one right after the other. There are times in our lives when a succession of things such as the death of a loved one, financial reversal, and health problems come so quickly that we keep our eyes on the horizon wondering if a cloud of locusts is moving our way.

I remember when we had three kids in diapers, the oldest needing extra medical attention. The church I pastored was building its first building. I ruptured a disc in my neck, and my wife developed mononucleosis. When things like this happen, you can't help but wonder, "Are we doing something wrong? How are we going to get through this?"

Do you assume you've done something wrong when suffering comes into your life? When storms come, it is important to remember that suffering itself is not a sign that God is angry with us. God was very pleased with Job. He was one of God's favorite people, and although we do sometimes suffer because we've done stupid or evil things, we will often suffer because we did the right thing.

Who shall separate us from the love of Christ?
Shall trouble or hardship or persecution or
famine or nakedness or danger or sword?

Romans 8:35

Godly Living

IN II TIMOTHY 3:12 WE READ, "everyone who wants to live a godly life in Christ Jesus will suffer persecution." He didn't say **might** suffer; he said **will suffer**. In Genesis 39, we read an especially poignant story that illustrates this truth:

Now Joseph had been taken down to Egypt. Potiphar, an Egyptian who was one of Pharaoh's officials, the captain of the guard, bought him from the Ishmaelites who had taken him there.

The Lord was with Joseph and he prospered, and he lived in the house of his Egyptian master. When his master saw that the Lord was with him and that the Lord gave him success in everything he did, Joseph found favor in his eyes and became his attendant. Potiphar put him in charge of his household, and he entrusted to his care everything he owned.

From the time he put him in charge of his household and of all that he owned, the Lord blessed the household of the Egyptian because of Joseph. The blessing of the Lord was on everything Potiphar had, both in the house and in the field.

So he left in Joseph's care everything he had; with Joseph in charge, he did not concern himself with anything except the food he ate. Now Joseph was well built and handsome, and after a while his master's wife took notice of Joseph and said, 'Come to bed with me!' But he refused.

'With me in charge,' he told her, 'my master does not concern himself with anything in the house; everything he owns he has entrusted to my care. No one is greater in this house than I am. My master has withheld nothing from me except you, because you are his wife. How then could I do such a wicked thing and sin against God?'

And though she spoke to Joseph day after day, he refused to go to bed with her or even be with her.

One day he went into the house to attend to his duties, and none of the household servants was inside.

She caught him by his cloak and said, 'Come to bed with me!' But he left his cloak in her hand and ran out of the house. When she saw that he had left his cloak in her hand and had run out of the house, she called her household servants.

'Look,' she said to them, 'this Hebrew has been brought to us to make sport of us! He came in here to sleep with me, but I screamed. When he heard me scream for help, he left his cloak beside me and ran out of the house.'

She kept his cloak beside her until his master came home. Then she told him this story: 'That Hebrew slave you brought us came to me to make sport of me. But as soon as I screamed for help, he left his cloak beside me and ran out of the house.'

When his master heard the story his wife told him, saying, 'This is how your slave treated me,' he burned with anger. Joseph's master took him and put him in prison, the place where the king's prisoners were confined.

But while Joseph was there in the prison, the Lord was with him; he showed him kindness and granted him favor in the eyes of the prison warden. So the warden put Joseph in charge of all those held in the prison, and he was made responsible for all that was done there. The warden paid no attention to anything under Joseph's care, because the Lord was with Joseph and gave him success in whatever he did.

JOSEPH DID THE RIGHT THING by refusing the advances of his boss's wife, and the result was a false accusation of attempted rape resulting in a prison sentence. He was suffering for righteousness sake. While he continued his righteous living in prison, it is certain that he found it difficult. Already a kidnap victim in a foreign land, he had gone from privileged son to hardworking slave. Now, he is imprisoned, surrounded by criminals and uncertain how he would ever regain his freedom.

The Bible is careful to repeatedly remind us that whenever we get in a situation where we suffer for doing the right thing, we should rejoice, considering ourselves especially blessed, remembering that persecution is the expectation of those who follow Christ. We're told, "Don't be surprised when you go through trials of various kinds."[9]

Suffering is not some strange aberrant thing in human existence. It is a normal part of the course of events. How you respond to suffering determines whether or not suffering will make you bitter or better. Will suffering make you more fragile or help you to become stronger?

Suffering is a reminder that sin has introduced death into God's created order. Suffering helps us to avoid becoming too attached to the things of this world. This world is not our home. In fact, the apostle Paul says in I Corinthians 15:19: "If only for this life we have hope in Christ, we are to be pitied more than all men."

When you're going through difficulty, you can run away from God, you can shake your fist at God, or you can open yourself up to God and say, "I can't be in control. I'm trusting you to do what's best to accomplish your purposes." If you're not prepared for the storms, you're going to be in big trouble, because **the storms are coming**. They may be physical, financial, relational or societal. As I deal with people going through all these different kinds of storms, I continually find that they seem utterly surprised when tragedy strikes them. Consider this a warning.

Physical Storms

Some people are determined to work hard to prevent tragedy in their lives. But, even if you exercise regularly and are careful with your diet, the person who is driving the car headed toward you may not be so careful. In fact, they may have had too much to drink, so their vehicle comes across the line and hits your car. All of a sudden, you may find that you're glad you ate right and exercised, because you have survived the accident, and now your physical stamina aids in a faster recovery. Even so, you come out of the accident very different. This happens to people everywhere every year. Are you prepared if it happens to you, your spouse or your child?

What happens if you find that you are genetically inclined toward a certain disease? Routine medical care, watching your diet and exercising faithfully hasn't made your pancreas willing to cooperate. Lots of people are diagnosed with diabetes every year. Some problems are so unusual that they make us feel as if we've been singled out for special trials.

I met a couple who were in their forties when the wife developed a pituitary tumor which caused an extremely rare medical condition making her grow several inches taller in a matter of months. Not only was this hard on her physically, but it changed her entire self-image and all of her relationships. This wasn't just a personal trauma; it affected every member of her extended family and all of their friendships as well.

We plan our future as if we're in control. While we may deceive ourselves for a while, we are never really in control. I remember going to the hospital to see a doctor because of a lump in the side of my neck. The doctor said I needed surgery, so I went for a second opinion. I've had eight surgeries, and I haven't looked forward to any of them. When I discovered the lump one morning while shaving, I was a busy pastor with three small children and a wife, all relying on me; I didn't have time to be sick.

When I went for a second opinion, I overheard a conversation as I sat in a crowd of people waiting to see the surgeon. A woman behind me was speaking to someone: "Excuse me. I see you have on a white uniform. Are you a nurse?"

"Yes," a distinctly female voice responded.

"Can I ask you a question?"

"Yes."

"What is oncology?"

"Oncology means cancer."

"That's what I thought," she said quietly.

Sitting there in the silence that followed, I began thinking, "Okay, I know I'm in the oncology ward, but that's because my brother is a cancer specialist and he knows people in this field. It's not because I have cancer. That couldn't happen to me."

I went in to see the doctor and the physician's assistant came, looked at my file, checked my neck and said, "Mr. Wood, I'm not clear why you're here. Were you looking for a second opinion or did you want Dr. Murray to do the surgery?"

I said, "I wanted a second opinion, and if I need surgery, I want him to do it."

She responded, "You definitely need surgery."

I thought, "I haven't even seen the doctor yet and she's telling me I *definitely* need surgery."

This was a Wednesday afternoon and she asked, "Will Friday be okay?"

I asked, "Is the doctor about to go out-of-town?"

She calmly but authoritatively said, "No."

I reluctantly responded, "Friday's fine."

When Dr. Murray came in, his extreme kindness to me made me feel much worse. Dr. Murray's manner and speech reminded me a great deal of Mr. Rogers of *Mr. Rogers' Neighborhood.* For some people this would have been reassuring, but I found it terrifying. He gently probed my neck and compassionately said, "We definitely need to get right at that." In that moment, I felt like a frightened child.

I thought, "Oh, I'm dead. I'll be dead for sure within three months. What will my wife and boys do?"

Dr. Murray proceeded to describe all the possible complications and ramifications of my surgery. "Reverend Wood, I should tell you that eighty percent of these tumors are benign. But, it goes without saying that if eighty percent are benign, that means twenty percent are not benign."

Inwardly I wanted to yell, "Yes, it goes without saying!" Yet, I knew that in our litigious society, a doctor has to cover all the bases.

The doctor then outlined the various types of malignancy, which might occur, and the various courses of treatment, which they would require. He described in detail the various types of nerve damage that could result from the surgery even if the tumor was benign.

Although I'm still here, the night before the surgery was a night I will never forget. The tumor was benign, but I was sweating bullets for a while. I know God has not promised anywhere in scripture, "Follow me and you will never go through difficulty. Follow me and you can't get cancer. Follow me and everything will be easy for you." No, God has promised that in this life, I will have tribulation, but he's also promised that he will always be there for me.

Again, I quote Paul, "If only for this life we have hope in Christ, we are to be pitied more than all men."[10] But thanks be to God, Jesus has risen from the dead. This world is not our home. We not only have the knowledge of God's presence in the present, we have the assurance of his promise for the future. When the storms come, we don't have to be afraid.

We all deal with the uncertainty of life, and we are all conditioned to fear certain storms on the horizon. Circumstances can change very rapidly. Not many years after my surgery, my wife went to a doctor in Knoxville who did an ultrasound and said, "You need to have surgery right away. You have some suspicious growths in your abdomen. In fact, it appears to be many growths that could be very serious."

The next day my wife was seeing the chief of gynecological oncology at Emory in Atlanta. His first message was, "I know your doctor seemed nervous, but there's not anything to be nervous about. You may not even need surgery. We'll run our own tests."

After the tests, the doctor came in and sat down silently. When my wife came in, he told us, "We need to do surgery as soon as possible." Those words sounded ominous.

God was merciful and all of the many tumors were benign. However, many of my friends, my age, have died in the last couple of years. Cancer, heart attack, and accidents take Christians, too. God never promised life would be easy or long. In fact, Jesus himself promised that in this world we will have trouble, but take heart, because Jesus also said, "I've already overcome the world."[11]

My great grandfather is famous in Wood family history for making an unusual comment during the nineteenth century Charleston earthquake. This particular ancestor was a congressman, well known for his distinguished bearing and his oratorical flourishes. As the house shook and the family began to realize it was an earthquake, my great grandfather proclaimed, "This is an earthquake! Isn't it sublime!"

My great grandfather knew that the Creator is in charge, and he was demonstrating his confidence in this knowledge. For the people whose roofs caved in on them, sublime may not have been the word that came to mind.

When you're in the midst of the storm, you can panic or you can turn your eyes to heaven. There is one who rules over all, and if I die, I'm in his hands. If I don't die, he has a purpose for me here. I don't have to be afraid.

Financial Storms

Financial storms will come. Sometimes they come because of our mistakes. People spend money they don't have. When some people lose financially, they really do lose everything of value to them. Instead of turning to God, they turn to alcohol or other drugs. They drink and drink and lose their business, homes, cars, collections, sobriety, and even their spouse and children.

Other people turn to the Lord when the financial storm comes. They cry out to God and yield their life to Christ. These people discover that money cannot give security. It can't give life meaning. It's not what gives purpose. It's not what gives people significance. Everything, including money, ultimately belongs to God. We are never more than stewards. Lazy or greedy stewards, perhaps, but stewards nonetheless.

When we comprehend that God owns everything and bow the knee to God's Sovereignty, we don't have to fear financial reversal. We must learn to depend on

God so that we can say with the apostle Paul, "I have learned the secret of being content in any and every situation, whether well fed or hungry, whether living in plenty or in want. I can do everything through him who gives me strength."[12]

When I left Atlanta to start the children's ministry in Tennessee, I had no promise of a pay check. I had to simply trust it was truly God leading me to start the ministry. After we had been in Wears Valley for several months, I had a conversation with a dear friend who was concerned for my welfare.

I told him, "This is the smallest amount of money I've made in many years, and it's the best off I've ever been financially."

He responded, "That's interesting. I just told my wife last week, 'This is the most money we've ever made in our lives and it's the worst off we've ever been financially.'"

It's not the amount of money coming in that determines your financial status. Trust in the Lord, and you never have to be afraid of the storm.

Relational Storms

Relational storms are inevitable. There will be difficulties in your relationships with others. You can't control other people, not even your spouse or your children. You may be able to cajole and manipulate, but ultimately you can't control other people. The most frustrated people are the control freaks who are determined to control others. It cannot be done. Accept the fact that you just can't control other people. It won't work.

So, what do you do if your spouse is unfaithful? What do you do if your spouse develops a problem with substance abuse? Can you *fix* them? No, you can't! You can't control them. The sooner you learn this, the better off you'll be. You can still love them. You're commanded to love. You can still forgive them. You're commanded to forgive, but don't try to control them. It won't work.

You don't have to trust them. Your responsibility is how you conduct yourself before God, not how they conduct themselves. If you feel responsible for what they do, you'll fail to do what you need to do. If you will focus on what God says you should be doing, you can live in peace and security. All you have to do is whatever God says to do. You can't get anyone else to do what's right for you. Each person will give an account to God.

I had a man talking to me recently on a cell phone in his driveway as his alcoholic wife tried to run him over. She wanted more liquor and he was trying to stop her from driving. He asked me, "What should I do?"

I said, "Call 911."

He asked, "What do you mean?"

I said, "Call 911." I pointed out to him, "She's a danger to herself and others."

He called 911.

What if it had been someone else trying to run over him? He wouldn't need to ask me what to do. He would know to call 911. If you see a drunk driver, report them please!

But, what if it's somebody you love? Be sure to dial the right number. You can't control that other person, even when you really love them. You can still do the right thing, even if they won't. While you can't control their behavior, you can seek to protect them and the other people in their path.

Societal Storms

What about societal problems? Political and economic changes occur in society beyond our control. These changes often have a direct impact on you, your marriage and your family. You need to learn how to deal with societal storms.

I remember when I was a kindergarten child in Villa Park, Illinois, and my fifteen-year-old sister wanted to tie up the bottom of a boy's shirt she was wearing. It was the fashion in the late nineteen fifties for girls to wear a long oxford shirt untucked and unbuttoned at the bottom and take the ends and tie them in a knot exposing the midriff. She was pleading with my dad after he told her to tuck the shirt in. She was assuring him that she had no intention of showing her midriff; she just wanted to tie the bottom so that she'd be in fashion.

While I was only five years old, I spoke up on behalf of my sister, "Dad I don't see what harm it would do."

Because I had spoken, Dad finally had a masculine figure to turn his wrath on. It's one of my most vivid childhood memories. His fifteen-year-old daughter had Dad wrapped around her little finger, and he was trying so hard to stand firm. When I spoke up, he had a male target. He could talk to a male in the tone that he wanted to use with my sister, so he turned on me and spoke in a way I'll never forget.

"You mark my words. By the time you have a fifteen-year-old daughter, she's going to be wanting to walk down the street wearing nothing but a brassiere up top." He had my full five-year-old attention.

However, Dad was inaccurate in his prophecy concerning the societal storm that was brewing. I didn't have a fifteen-year-old daughter when his prophecy was realized; I was only fifteen myself. Halter-tops were the rage within ten years of that confrontation. Dad was right about the direction of our society. He just couldn't have imagined how fast things were sliding downhill.

When the storms invade your home, you need to be prepared. You can't start preparing after the storm hits. And, you don't want to be left with nothing but broken lives.

Kyle Matthews is a gifted songwriter and a dear friend. One of his songs, **The Rain is Coming**, captures the essence of the reality of Jesus' words concerning the storms that will come into all our lives:

The Rain is Coming

**The rain is coming into your life
The rain is coming you can't hide
The winds are gonna blow
The thunder's gonna roll
And lightning will fill the sky**

**The rain is coming from the coast
It is the storm you fear the most
You can run for help
But you cannot save yourself
You never could, you know**

"I'll never leave you. Don't let the storm deceive you. I can see you through these days. This is the promise. You have to build upon it, and keep your love for me from being washed away." [13]

Ready or not, the storms are coming! Your marriage and family can grow stronger as you endure the storms, or you can have your most important relationships washed away. Are you prepared?

One day Jesus said to his disciples, 'Let's go over to the other side of the lake.' So, they got into a boat and set out.

As they sailed, he fell asleep. A squall came down on the lake, so that the boat was being swamped, and they were in great danger.

The disciples went and woke him, saying, 'Master, Master, we're going to drown!' He got up and rebuked the wind and the raging waters; the storm subsided, and all was calm.

'Where is your faith?' he asked his disciples.

In fear and amazement, they asked one another, 'Who is this? He commands even the winds and the water, and they obey him.'

Luke 8:22-25.

Jesus, why are you sleeping?

HAVE YOU EVER BEEN IN THIS BOAT? It seems like Jesus is sleeping. You know he's with you, but he must be asleep. These disciples had seen Jesus do all kinds of miracles, but during the storm, they needed him to be awake. Many of these men were seasoned fisherman, comfortable on the water most of the time. Jesus had told them to get into the boat, and Jesus had gone to sleep. Now, a storm was raging and they felt abandoned.

53

God was there with them bodily and yet they still felt abandoned. We're not alone in our feelings of abandonment when the storms come. David, the psalmist, describes this feeling repeatedly. He often points out his problems to the Lord clearly feeling that God must be unaware. We often address God as if he needs us to explain the gravity of our situation.

Was the situation in this story serious? The boat was being swamped. They were going under. They were in great danger, not just the potential for possible harm. So, why did Jesus ask them, "Where's your faith?"

If you want to understand verse twenty-five, you have to go back to verse twenty-two. Jesus asks in twenty-five, "Where's your faith?" But, in verse twenty-two Jesus had said, "Let's go over to the other side of the lake."

If Jesus says, "Let's go over to the other side of the lake," they're going to make it to the other side of the lake. We understand this intellectually. And, these men had already seen Jesus' word come true repeatedly, but their faith wasn't in his word during the storm. When the storm came, they got their eyes focused on the circumstances. Suddenly, they were panicked. The boat was being swamped. They were in great danger.

If their current circumstances were all they knew, they had every reason to be afraid. But, Jesus was teaching them that there is something that is supposed to be much more real to us than the wind and the waves and the immediate situation. If they had simply reached back and held on to what Jesus had already said, they would have had calm in the storm.

Jesus was really asleep. Sometimes, in our determination to remember that Jesus is God(who never sleeps), we forget that Jesus is also fully man. He got hungry, tired, and sleepy, so he ate and slept. In this dire situation, Jesus was really asleep. But, though Jesus was sleeping, it didn't change the word that had already been spoken. Even as he slept, the truthfulness of his word was not compromised. Though the circumstances were terrifying, his word had already been pronounced. And Jesus' word transcends time and difficulty. At Jesus' word, the dead come back to life: "Lazarus come forth."[14]

Jesus spoke the world into being. If we trust in his word, we can say what he tells us to say, and we can be sure it will happen. He doesn't simply offer to cause anything that we want to happen. He promises that if we believe his word and abide in his word and his word abides in us, then we can ask whatever we will and it will be done.[15]

I can relate to these disciples. I have been in situations where I was distracted from what God had promised by what I was feeling, seeing, and tasting. The word of God has sometimes become very small while my circumstances grew very large. With this false perception came fear, instability, and a readiness to sin. We're much more vulnerable to sin, once we stop trusting God. The response of the disciples was fear and amazement, not relief and delight. In fear and amazement, after the storm subsides they ask each other, "Who is this? Even the winds and the sea obey him."

Earlier, we said that obedience to God's word is the key to building a solid foundation for our lives. The key to having peace in the storm is also obedience to God's word. The reason the disciples panicked was because they failed to continue in obedient faith. They had started out obeying him. They got into the boat at his command, but the subsequent tough circumstances overwhelmed their emotions. Relying on feelings rather than God's word was a problem for them, just as it is for us today. Therefore, their response was fear, instead of the peace God offers.

It is comforting to know that Jesus had to repeatedly teach this same lesson to his closest disciples throughout his ministry. In Matthew 14:22-33, we read a similar story with a similar outcome:

Immediately Jesus made the disciples get into the boat and go on ahead of him to the other side, while he dismissed the crowd.

After he had dismissed them, he went up on a mountainside by himself to pray. When evening came, he was there alone, but the boat was already a considerable distance from land, buffeted by the waves because the wind was against it.

During the fourth watch of the night, Jesus went out to them, walking on the lake. When the disciples saw him walking on the lake, they were terrified. 'It's a ghost,' they said, and cried out in fear.

But Jesus immediately said to them: 'Take courage! It is I. Don't be afraid.'

'Lord, if it's you,' Peter replied, 'tell me to come to you on the water.'

'Come,' he said. Then Peter got down out of the boat, walked on the water and came toward Jesus.

But when he saw the wind, he was afraid and, beginning to sink, cried out, 'Lord, save me!'

Immediately Jesus reached out his hand and caught him. 'You of little faith,' he said, 'why did you doubt?'

And when they climbed into the boat, the wind died down. Then those who were in the boat worshiped him, saying, 'Truly you are the Son of God.'

BOTH STORIES INVOLVE JESUS and his disciples in a boat on a lake during a storm. In both cases, Jesus is teaching them the same lesson. Why was Peter able to walk on the water? Jesus said, "Come." It only took one word from Jesus. If Jesus says, "Come," you can walk on the water. If Jesus says, "Let's go to the other side," you can go to the other side. Regardless of the circumstances, you can do whatever Jesus tells you to do. If we really believe what Jesus says, we can do seemingly impossible things.

When Susan and I told our church in Atlanta that we were leaving in order to move to the mountains and start a children's home, people were desperately trying to figure out what must have had happened. Had I had an affair? Was this burnout? Was their some financial scandal? What's going on? People don't leave a comfortable and prosperous situation in order to go to a situation requiring a miracle just to make life bearable. You certainly don't launch a ministry in another state where you are completely unknown during a recession. 1991 was not the best time to be starting a new venture in ministry. But, it was God's time. He delights in making his involvement unmistakable.

If we look at circumstances and try to discern God's will on that basis, we sometimes get it right. But, there's a strong likelihood that we're going to get it wrong. God is forever in the business of doing the impossible. God delights in manifesting his strength in the context of our weakness. Over and over, God put his disciples in situations where the only thing they could rely upon was what he had said to them.

In verse twenty-two of Matthew 14, Jesus made the disciples go on ahead of him to the other side. He had told them what to do, so they set out to obey. But then, a major storm came up some time between three and six a.m. John tells us that the waters were rough, and the wind was strong. They were tired, frustrated and scared. Then, along came Jesus. Mark includes the humorous fact that Jesus acted as if he was about to pass them by. They were straining at the oars, and Jesus is strolling past them.

Instead of saying, "Oh wonderful! Jesus is here;" they said, "It's a ghost!" Often, when Jesus begins to work in our lives, especially in the middle of a storm, we misunderstand what's going on, and we think things are getting worse instead of better.

Paul and Silas were in the Philippian jail. They had been wrongly accused and beaten illegally. They were in the least desirable innermost cell with their ankles and wrists manacled and their backs bleeding from beatings. They were in pain! Around midnight, it was dark, but they couldn't sleep.

I imagine Silas said to Paul, "Is there anything we can be thankful for?"

Paul responded, "Yes. It can't get any worse."

As they began to sing praises to God, an earthquake hit. God didn't send a warning ahead of the earthquake. He didn't tell them that it would turn out for their good. As they were singing praises, the ground began to shake and a loud rumble filled the dark, smelly enclosure.

About midnight, Paul and Silas were praying and singing hymns to God, and the other prisoners were listening to them.

Suddenly there was such a violent earthquake that the foundations of the prison were shaken. At once all the prison doors flew open, and everybody's chains came loose. [16]

We can be determined in a difficult trying time that we're just going to praise God. We can stand against the devil by praising and worshipping God, not because we feel like it, but because it's the right thing to do. Then, something else happens that seems even worse. It makes it hard not to cry out, "God, where are you? Don't you see what I'm going through? Are you asleep? Do you just not care?" It is in times like these that God is teaching his children to trust him.

Jesus did things that terrified his disciples, but it wasn't because he wanted them to be terrified, it was because he wanted to teach them not to be terrified. He put them into terrifying situations, so they could learn that when things seem terrifying, God can still be trusted.

We have the advantage of seeing the future of these disciples, and we know now that they obviously needed this preparation. They didn't know that this was only the beginning of much worse things to come. They spoke to officials giving testimony to the fact that Jesus Christ is alive. They preached to hostile crowds who ultimately killed them. They would eventually be martyred for their faith in God. God graciously prepared them through tough circumstances, because he loved them.

We often feel that God doesn't love us, when he is doing things to demonstrate how much he loves us. He toughens us up and teaches us to trust him in the midst of the storm. This is where real peace comes from. "Peace that passes understanding"[17] is a peace not easily understood. It's a peace that doesn't make sense to those without Christ, because the situation seems to be crying out for great anxiety and fear. Jesus wants us to have peace in him. He said, "I have told you these things, so that in me you may have peace. In this world you will have trouble. But take heart! I have overcome the world."[18]

These words weren't just for first century disciples. These words are also for us. We're still facing tough situations. He has promised us the same trouble he promised them. But, he's also promised us the same peace he promised them. God sees the end of the story and how even the most difficult things will be used for good.

The most difficult situations I have faced in learning to trust God have involved our oldest son Paul and his medical needs stemming from his birth defect,

Spina Bifida. Just before his second birthday, we went through an excruciatingly painful time with him.

Paul had twelve shunt failures in the span of two weeks. A shunt is a tube that carries blocked cerebral spinal fluid from the brain and into the abdomen. This enables the brain to function. When the shunt fails, the person has horrible headaches, then projectile vomiting, loss of consciousness, and if the problem is not corrected, the person eventually dies. Paul had severe shunt failure twelve times over a period of two weeks. The doctors did numerous invasive procedures to unblock it, including four brain surgeries.

During this same time, our car broke down. I was the new pastor of a new church start on Cape Cod over two hours away from Boston and the hospital. It's always difficult to launch a new church, but doing it two hours from where your child has to be rushed to the hospital, and your car breaks down, can lead you to believe that God isn't paying attention.

Certainly, God showed us kindness during these difficult days. My brother loaned us his car while ours was being repaired and offered to pay for our transmission to be replaced. Still, difficulties kept recurring. One Sunday afternoon at a church picnic and baptismal service, we noticed that Paul was becoming increasingly lethargic. We headed home praying that his shunt wasn't blocked again. When the projectile vomiting began, we rushed Paul to the car and headed for Boston.

As we headed to Children's Hospital in my brother's car, the traffic was unbelievable. It was the last weekend of the summer tourist season, and there were multiple lanes of traffic lined up to merge and cross a two-lane bridge. The traffic was backed up so badly that our two-hour trip became a five-hour trip, while Paul was literally dying.

When we finally got to the bridge, there was a policeman directing traffic. I told him we had a medical emergency and asked if he could radio for help. He said we would be better off to just keep driving. There was nothing he could do to help.

Several miles later, we began to pick up speed and were about half an hour out of Boston when a railroad tie fell off the back of a truck in front of us, rolled down the interstate and blew out one of our tires. While we were grateful to be uninjured, now we were broken down in a borrowed car on the side of the interstate in the pitch black dark.

As a steady stream of cars passed by, I tried to flag someone down to give us a ride to Children's Hospital. Finally, Susan called to me and asked me to get back in the car while she tried to get someone to stop. She ran back down the interstate and a car stopped almost immediately.

A young man in a two-door sports coupe took us to Children's in record time. We ran through the corridors of the hospital, and Paul was in surgery within twenty minutes of our arrival.

While I dealt with the admission's office and cared for our infant son Clayton, Susan was rocking Paul and singing to him in the hallway as the doctors were being paged for surgery. One of the other parents on the neurological floor stepped out into the hall and said to Susan, "How can you seem so happy and peaceful when your son is going through this suffering?" He didn't ask in a compassionate voice, though his sincerity was plain. It turned out that he had been watching for two weeks as we repeatedly brought Paul to the hospital for surgeries and procedures.

Most of the time when you're going through trials, it's hard to see anything but the circumstances. The other people with children on Division 33 saw our circumstances too, and they saw a different response to the stress and pain in our lives. In the midst of the storm, there was a peace, a calm, and a joy.

The man who asked Susan the question became a believer that night. During the night, he went through deliverance and the most painful struggle of his life; then, he gave his life to Christ.

Throughout all of my son's surgeries, we have seen the faithfulness of God. He has used those most difficult times in order to bring tremendous blessings into our lives. We continue to receive letters from that man almost twenty years after this encounter. He and his family are still our friends, faithful followers of Christ and part of God's family forever.

We recently received a photo of his family, including their son who had had an inoperable brain tumor that had taken his vision at age six. After his conversion, his wife, his daughter, and over thirty members of his extended family all came to Jesus. God saved his six-year-old son, and not only did the boy live, his sight was miraculously restored.

God has worked tremendous blessings in the lives of so many people through intense suffering. We have precious relationships with people that were forged on the anvil of pain. Because we were hurting and they were hurting, God brought us together with a common bond. It gave us a way of relating to each other. These people would have never listened to what we had to say about our loving heavenly Father, except for the fact that they could see joy and peace in the midst of our own pain and suffering.

I remember sitting in a backyard swing with Susan during one of our rare times of quiet together during Paul's weeks of surgeries. I was thoroughly exhausted and discouraged because my hopes were ignited then doused repeatedly within short stretches of time. I was distracted by the circumstances.

We had finally given up returning to our home on Cape Cod and had brought our infant son Clayton to a friend's home near the hospital. That way we could go back and forth between our children.

Despairingly, I said to Susan, "I think I could handle it if God were to say that he were going to take Paul, and I would be so grateful if God would just heal Paul. But, this not knowing hurts too much."

Susan responded, "God hasn't promised that we'll make it back to the hospital to visit Paul this evening. We could be killed in a car wreck. He hasn't said that Clayton will live to be as old as Paul is now. Life is about learning to trust God in any and every situation. This is a great opportunity to grow deeper in our trust and dependence on God."

God is bigger than any problem we face. And, God doesn't say, "If you trust and obey, everything will be pleasant." God says, "I have a crown laid up for you and you will receive rewards for your faithfulness." Jesus never promised it would be easy, but he promised that he has a plan. When the storm comes, if we focus on the circumstances, we are in trouble. But, if when the storm comes, we lay hold of his word, and say, "No matter what happens, I know God's word is true and I can trust him," then we have peace in the midst of the storm.

The apostle Paul understood this. He spent a lot of time in prison. In fact, much of the New Testament was written in a prison cell. Paul says in Romans 8:

What then shall we say in response to this? If God is for us, who can be against us? He who did not spare his own son, but gave him up for us all, how will he not also along with him graciously give us all things? Who will bring any charge against those God has chosen? It is God who justifies. Who is he that condemns? Christ Jesus who died, more than that, who was raised to life, is at the right hand of God and is also interceding for us. Who shall separate us from the love of Christ? Shall trouble or hardship or persecution or famine or nakedness or danger or sword? As it is written, 'for your sake we face death all day long. We are considered as sheep to be slaughtered.' No, in all these things we are more than conquerors through him who loved us. For I am convinced that neither death nor life, neither angels nor demons, neither the present nor the future nor any powers, neither height nor depth, nor anything else in all creation will be able to separate us from the love of God that is in Christ Jesus our Lord.

THIS IS WHAT WE hold onto in the storm. This is what we cling to when the waves are breaking over our boat and the boat is filling with water. We cling to the promise of one who can take us for a walk on the water, if that's what's needed. When he says we're going to the other side, we can count on it. Where is your faith? This is what Jesus is asking. Are we willing to trust him? If we trust him, we'll have peace while the storm is raging.

Praise be to the God and Father of our Lord
Jesus Christ! In his great mercy he has given us
new birth into a living hope through the
resurrection of Jesus Christ from the dead, and
into an inheritance that can never perish, spoil
or fade—kept in heaven for you, who through
faith are shielded by God's power until the
coming of the salvation that is ready to be
revealed in the last time.

In this, you greatly rejoice, though now for a
little while you may have had to suffer grief in
all kinds of trials. These have come so that your
faith—of greater worth than gold, which
perishes even though refined by fire—may be
proved genuine and may result in praise, glory
and honor when Jesus Christ is revealed.

Though you have not seen him, you love him;
and even though you do not see him now, you
believe in him and are filled with an
inexpressible and glorious joy, for you are
receiving the goal of your faith, the salvation of
your souls.

1 Peter 1:3-9.

Growing stronger in the storms

IN THESE VERSES, PETER tells a group of people who are in the midst of real suffering that their faith is more precious than gold. Even though the fire refines gold, gold is not eternal. When the advertisers tell us that "a diamond is forever," that's hyperbole. A diamond lasts a long time, but it's not forever. Our salvation, however, is forever. God is at work refining us, so we come out shining like gold, reflecting the glory of his light. Our lives become purer, better, and stronger as a result of his work in us in the midst of suffering. It is when we go through difficulty that what's inside comes to the surface. The refining process involves heating metal and as it is heated, hidden impurities rise to the surface. The dross has to be removed time and time again. A refiner knows the process is complete when he can see his reflection in the metal.

When things in our lives get tough, our attitude rises to the surface. The dross is revealed in our vocabulary perhaps or our lack of patience. We might think we had really changed, and in the heat of tough times, we find some of the old dross was still inside. God brings this to the surface, not because he doesn't love us, but because he loves us so much. He wants to remove the impurities from our lives until, in the midst of our affliction, we are worshipping and praising him. This isn't cruelty on God's part; it's compassion, because he's fitting us for heaven. He's preparing us for an eternity of praise, worship and devoted service.

What Peter describes is the way God's power shields us as we are going through great difficulty. We are called to live in anticipation of the fullness of salvation that we will experience when Jesus draws us together and there will be no more pain, suffering and no more goodbyes. He says, "Though now for a little while, you may have had to suffer grief in all kinds of trials . . ." it's only for a little while. When you're in the middle of pain, it seems like it is lasting forever. When you're hurting, time stands still. It feels unbearable, because it feels like it's going to last forever. It's not!

Our sufferings in this life are temporary. If we know this and learn in the midst of our suffering to trust in the one who is still in control, knowing that only what he allows can happen, we actually grow stronger in the storm. Our faith is developed, not diminished. It's purified, not destroyed.

Joseph Tson is a Romanian pastor who suffered greatly under communist persecution. He testifies that God said to him about his persecutors, "These people are like puppets. You need to realize that even though the things they do to you hurt, I am working for your good. I am working in this situation to bless you." This is hard for us to understand, but the thing God is teaching is our need to ultimately trust and depend on him, knowing that his heart is tender and compassionate toward us.

This came home to me most profoundly as a father with a son who needed surgery. There was no way for me to explain to Paul why the doctors were doing what they were doing. Yet, even when they were working to save his life, as a small child Paul would cry out and look to me as if to say, "Why don't you do something? Why don't you stop these men from hurting me?" I couldn't explain it to him. When I said, "These men are helping you," it made no sense to him at all. But I knew that it was because of my love for him that I held him still while doctors and nurses worked on him. It wasn't because I didn't love him. I loved him so much that I held him still while painful things happened. It tore me up to see him hurt. Yet, I loved him enough to allow him to go through the pain in order to give him better health long-term. I wanted him to have greater strength and more options to more effectively serve the Lord.

In James 1:2-8 we see the same theme:

> Consider it pure joy, my brothers, whenever you face trials of many kinds, because you know that the testing of your faith develops perseverance. Perseverance must finish its work so that you may be mature and complete, not lacking anything.

> If any of you lacks wisdom, he should ask God, who gives generously to all without finding fault, and it will be given to him. But when he asks, he must believe and not doubt, because he who doubts is like a wave of the sea, blown and tossed by the wind. That man should not think he will

receive anything from the Lord; he is a double-minded man, unstable in all he does.

These verses were not written by a pampered celebrity working on his next Christian bestseller, poolside in some resort. This is God's word given to us through a man who knew painful suffering. When we go through suffering, we are to consider it pure joy. This is God's command. How many times do we want to have to take the course in order to learn this vital lesson?

One of my boys said recently, "Dad I'm feeling convicted that I should pay you back for any course that I didn't make an A in while in college." As you might imagine, it was an idea that had a certain amount of appeal. But, I assured him that I was happy to pay for his courses; I just want him to do his best.

We did have an understanding with the boys that we'd pay for their courses once. If they needed to take a course again, they could pay. Our motive was to motivate them. God doesn't want us to have to take the course over and over again. Yet, it is necessary for us to go through trials in order to develop perseverance and perseverance will finish its work so that we might be mature and complete.

Our Lord Jesus, who was sinless, had to be made perfect and complete through the things that he suffered. Otherwise, he couldn't be our high priest. We have a high priest who is able to identify with us in all things. He has been tempted in all things just as we are, yet without sin.

If Jesus had to undergo difficulty in order to be perfect and complete as our high priest, should we wonder that his word is true when he says, "If this is the way they treated me, this is the way they're going to treat you. A servant is not above his teacher." Paul prayed, "I want to know Christ and the power of his resurrection and the fellowship of sharing in his sufferings, becoming like him in his death. . ."[19]

This has been my life's prayer since I was a teenager. I want to know him and the power of his resurrection. But, with this comes the fellowship of his sufferings, even being conformed to the likeness of his death. I don't always like the way this feels, but I am grateful that when sorrows and difficulties come, I know there is a Sovereign God on the throne who is allowing these things in my life, not because he can't control everything, but because he wants to bless me. I don't always feel like it. It often doesn't make sense to me. But, instead of letting circumstances be the deciding factor in whether or not I'm doing okay, I'm learning to keep my eyes fixed on Jesus and to hold on to the word he has given in scripture.

If I depend on circumstances, there will be tremendous instability and as James says, I will become a double-minded person, not even sure if I really want the will of God. When James speaks of praying for wisdom, he is telling us to pray that we might have God's perspective. God doesn't share his perspective with people who are not committed to doing his will. Do you want God's perspective so that you can obey, or do you want God's perspective so that you can consider that as one of your options?

Often we want God to give us wisdom, but what we really want is for God to show us his perspective and we'll weigh and consider it. If it's too costly, we aren't ready to obey. God doesn't offer wisdom this way. God says he gives wisdom generously to those who aren't double minded, those who have already made up their minds to do whatever God says, whatever the cost.

In Hebrews 12: 1-11, we read:

Therefore, since we are surrounded by such a great cloud of witnesses, let us throw off everything that hinders and the sin that so easily entangles, and let us run with perseverance the race marked out for us.

Let us fix our eyes on Jesus, the author and perfecter of our faith, who for the joy set before him endured the cross, scorning its shame, and sat down at the right hand of the throne of God.

Consider him who endured such opposition from sinful men, so that you will not grow weary and lose heart. In your struggle against sin, you have not yet resisted to the point of shedding your blood. And you have forgotten that word of encouragement that addresses you as sons: 'My son, do not make light of the Lord's discipline, and do not lose heart when he rebukes you, because the Lord disciplines those he loves, and he punishes everyone he accepts as a son.'

Endure hardship as discipline; God is treating you as sons. For what son is not disciplined by his father? If you are not disciplined (and every one undergoes discipline) then you are illegitimate children and not true sons. Moreover, we have all had human fathers who disciplined us and we respected them for it. How much more should we submit to the Father of our spirits and live!

Our fathers disciplined us for a little while as they thought best; but God disciplines us for our good, that we may share in his holiness.

No discipline seems pleasant at the time, but painful. Later on, however, it produces a harvest of righteousness and peace for those who have been trained by it.

No discipline seems pleasant at the time. If it's pleasant, it's not discipline. Discipline is painful, later on, however, it produces a harvest of righteousness and peace *for those who have been trained by it.* This last phrase indicates that some people go through discipline, and they don't learn. They're not trained by it, so they have to take the course over and over again.

If, as you go through discipline, you are trained by it, there will be great reward and great results. God doesn't delight in our pain; rather, God is allowing pain and difficulty in our lives in order that we might know him better, trust him more and reflect his glory. His power is made perfect in our weakness. When we are weak, he is strong.

Knowing this does not mean that we understand all there is to know about God and how he governs. But, it does mean that when we're going through a storm, when the waves are crashing over our boat and it's filling with water and we can see the great danger, we know we're not alone in the boat. And, there is one who has already said, "We're going to the other side."

Jesus says in John 14:8: "I go to prepare a place for you. If I go, I will come again so that you can be with me forever." This is the plan, and God always keeps his promises. He always does what he says he will do. We grow stronger in the storms if, when the suffering is greatest, we draw close to God, not saying, "God make it stop;" but saying, "God make me like you."

Part of the fruit of the Holy Spirit is long-suffering. Someone has said, "The only way to learn long-suffering is by suffering long." Sometimes we look at other people's lives and think, "I don't get it. Why are things always so good for them? Why don't they ever have to suffer?" But, we don't know what they're going through. The people who come to me after I speak and say, "What you described is exactly what I'm going through", always amaze me. I would never have guessed they had had these struggles and painful experiences from outward appearances.

At the conferences where I speak, everyone comes together and has a great time. There is always lots of joking and affection. But, every single person at every conference and in every church where I have ever preached has dealt with suffering and pain. We're not always going through pain personally, but whenever anyone we love is hurting, we hurt too.

Whatever kind of difficulty we go through, we must remember that it is temporary, and God is working for our good. We're not going to hurt forever. We're not going to feel alone forever. God is at work in the midst of our pain in order to fit us for glory. He will be successful. We're not in charge of this process, and neither is the devil. God, the Sovereign gracious Lord, is working in your life to bring about your good and his glory. We need to believe this. This is how we grow stronger in the midst of the storm.

We built our home in Tennessee on the side of a mountain. The view is always tremendous, but it is best after a storm. The air is clearer, and our vision is extended. I have seen this principle in other circumstances as well. Numerous cancer patients have told me that their illness gave them a brand new appreciation for life, their family, and their faith. Accident victims and people who have suffered great financial reversals have expressed deep gratitude for lessons learned.

A family who lived near the academy where Susan and I taught when we were first married narrowly escaped when their home burned to the ground. The wife showed great wisdom when she said, "If I had come home from the store and found my house was gone, I would have said, 'we lost everything.' But, having escaped with our lives, I realize that we lost nothing of value. Everything else we can replace or live without. I thank God for showing us what's really important."

When the storm is so dark that you cannot see past the end of your boat, remember, "This is temporary. God is in control. Whatever happens, those who love God will benefit from this trial." Then, be sure that you are in the group that benefits. God wants to give you his strength in the midst of your weakness. When the clouds lift, you'll find that the view is grand!

Praise be to the God and Father of our Lord Jesus Christ, the Father of compassion and the God of all comfort, who comforts us in all our troubles, so that we can comfort those in any trouble with the comfort we ourselves have received from God.

For just as the sufferings of Christ flow over into our lives, so also through Christ our comfort overflows.

If we are distressed, it is for your comfort and salvation; if we are comforted, it is for your comfort, which produces in you patient endurance of the same sufferings we suffer.

And our hope for you is firm, because we know that just as you share in our sufferings, so also you share in our comfort.

2 Corinthians 1: 3-7.

Religion that God our Father accepts as pure and faultless is this: to look after orphans and widows in their distress and to keep oneself from being polluted by the world.

James 1:27

Blessing others in the Storms

GOD IS IN THE PROCESS of making us one with each other, binding our lives together. When we go through difficulty, we can either grow further apart or closer together. The tragedy is that many people grow further apart. God has called us to draw closer to one another when times are tough. Within the body of Christ, when one member suffers, it is the responsibility of the other members to come alongside and provide comfort and encouragement.

The word that Paul uses for comfort is not a word we would associate with a pillow. It is a word that has to do with one who comes alongside us to help us on the journey. It is the encouragement provided by a companion, the Holy Spirit of our Risen Lord who gives strong support, strength in the midst of weakness. This is the kind of comfort Paul is speaking of. This is how God comforts us in our troubles, so that we can comfort those in any trouble. We don't have to have endured the exact same problem as someone else in order to come alongside them to empathize and commiserate.

The goal is not to share with a hurting person how much greater our problems are. We want to come alongside them and say, "I am so sorry you're going through this. Thank you for letting me know what's happening. I want you to know that I want to be here for you. Please, let me know what I can do to help." Often, those simple words of comfort are the greatest aid we can give. In fact, sometimes the silent presence of one who realizes they don't know what to say is the most comforting. But, we need to pray and look for other ways to help as well.

God will bring into your life people who have hurts similar to yours. I heard a testimony from a thirty-year-old woman who came from a very difficult background. Nobody knew what had been going on in her family throughout her childhood. She was on a mission's trip when she was in her late teens, and she met a young girl who was involved in some very self-destructive behavior. As she tried to talk with the girl about God and the fact that God loved her, the girl said, "I can't believe there is a God who loves me."

She asked, "Why?"

The young girl said, "My father molested me. How could God let something like that happen?"

This older teen said, "I'm going to tell you something I've never told anybody before. I've had to deal with the same problem. My father had sex with me."

This young woman said that as she talked with that girl, for the first time in her life, she began to understand that God had allowed her to go through something unspeakably horrible so that she would be able to share the gospel with others. She said, "What I never could have imagined in my pain is that God would open the door for me to share with many, many other teenage girls and young women who are suffering with the scars of sexual abuse. I would never have been able to share the gospel in the way that I have if it weren't for the fact that I've been through what they've been through. I understand their pain. I can talk with them in a way that they can hear and receive the healing power of the gospel of God's grace and love for them."

God isn't the author of sin. He doesn't cause people to do bad things. But, God is so infinitely wise, powerful and gracious that he can take the most horrible things that have ever happened and bring good out of them.

When we celebrate Good Friday, we're celebrating the worst thing that has ever happened on our planet. The most hideously evil event occurred when the sinless Son of God was nailed to a cross. The only one who had lived a perfect life was unjustly treated and killed. Yet, he said, "No one takes it [my life] from me, but I lay it down of my own accord. I have authority to lay it down and authority to take it up again. This command I received from my Father."[20]

Because he suffered and died, salvation is offered to us. This is the one we worship. He didn't just come and talk to us about suffering. He came alongside us and did what needed to be done. He provided his life. When we celebrate the Lord's Supper, we are remembering that, because of his brokenness, we can be made whole. Because his blood was poured out, our sins are washed away. God is always in the process of taking whatever we do and whatever is done to us and turning it for our good. When we believe what God says, it changes everything for us.

Jesus said, 'I am the true vine, and my Father is the gardener. He cuts off every branch in me that bears no fruit, while every branch that does bear fruit, he prunes so that it will be even more fruitful.

....

I am the vine; you are the branches. If a man remains in me and I in him, he will bear much fruit; apart from me, you can do nothing. If anyone does not remain in me, he is like a branch that is thrown away and withers; such branches are picked up, thrown into the fire and burned.

If you remain in me and my words remain in you, ask whatever you wish, and it will be given you. This is to my Father's glory, that you bear much fruit, showing yourselves to be my disciples.'[21]

If you are experiencing pruning, it is so that you might bless others. It's so that you might bear more fruit. It's not a sign that God is finished with you. It's not an indication that God is displeased with you. It is a reminder that God *isn't finished* with us. So, the apostle Paul says in II Cor. 4:7-18:

But we have this treasure in jars of clay to show that this all-surpassing power is from God and not from us.

We are hard pressed on every side, but not crushed; perplexed, but not in despair; persecuted, but not abandoned; struck down, but not destroyed.

We always carry around in our body the death of Jesus, so that the life of Jesus may also be revealed in our body.

For we who are alive are always being given over to death for Jesus' sake, so that his life may be revealed in our mortal body.

So then, death is at work in us, but life is at work in you.

It is written: 'I believed; therefore I have spoken.' With that same spirit of faith we also believe and therefore speak, because we know that the one who raised the Lord Jesus from the dead will also raise us with Jesus and present us with you in his presence.

All this is for your benefit, so that the grace that is reaching more and more people may cause thanksgiving to overflow to the glory of God.

Therefore, we do not lose heart. Though outwardly we are wasting away, yet inwardly we are being renewed day by day.

For our light and momentary troubles are achieving for us an eternal glory that far outweighs them all. So, we fix our eyes not on what is seen, but on what is unseen, for what is seen is temporary, but what is unseen is eternal.

It's your decision whether or not you will focus your attention on things that are eternal. You are not in danger of becoming "so heavenly minded that you are of no earthly good." In fact, it is the person whose mindset is focused on eternity who is able to live strategically in this present life. If we really believe that heaven is our home, then we begin to gain an understanding of our mission here on earth. The result is a life invested in others. Cities and civilizations crumble; people will live for eternity. Therefore, we must invest in people in ways that will impact their eternal destiny.

Climate Control

IF WE'RE GOING to make a difference in the lives of others, we need to start at home. There are times when the problems of this world seem overwhelming. There are times when we are tempted to think that there is no way for us to make a difference.

In reality, God has not given us responsibility for running this planet, much less the universe. He does hold us accountable, however, for how we govern those areas we can control.

You are only responsible for the stewardship that God gives you. How much impact you can have in your home depends upon your position in the home—parent, child, husband or wife. It also depends on the cooperation of the other members of the household. If your mate is uncooperative, don't despair. Don't get "stressed out" if the atmosphere in your home is not all that you believe it should be. But, if you are not doing what God commands, don't blame it on your family. Just as you can't control them, they don't control you. You will be held responsible for your attitudes and actions. Simply do what God allows and leave the rest to him.

Earlier in this book, I spoke of the importance of building on a solid foundation. I want to continue that metaphor, because it is scriptural and because the parallels are obvious. Realize that the decisions you make have consequences. Every day, you experience the results of past decisions. Each day offers the opportunity to build a better tomorrow.

God's desire is that your life would bear testimony to his grace. He wants you not only to survive the storms, but also to have a life that provides safety and stability to others. You can only experience this kind of life as you obey God's direction. You will find more often than not that following Jesus means behaving differently than the world around you. Your home should be a lighthouse in the darkness.

Many of us who grew up in Christian homes are all too familiar with the temptation to focus on appearances without really dealing with what's going on inside. Like the Pharisees, we make sure the outside of the dish is clean, but inside there's a mess.[22] God wants you to yield your life and your home to him. He wants his character to be reflected in your relationships. He wants his presence to set the atmosphere in your home.

Climate-control is essential, but it is also costly! We cannot allow conditions outside our home to determine the atmosphere inside. It's not enough to have insulation. We've got to have a way to regulate the atmosphere inside. It takes energy to regulate the atmosphere. Let's apply the metaphor.

There are going to be all kinds of pressures vying for our attention — at home, at church, at work, at school, issues in the media, culture wars, people denying the truth. It thrills me when I hear of someone who is responsibly establishing and enforcing God-given priorities. When I hear a man or woman say they have changed jobs because their job was negatively affecting their family life, I thank God that there are still people who are determined not to let the world squeeze them into its mold. When they are being pressured to compromise, they call upon the Holy Spirit's power and break free. They are saying that their family is more important than their job, and they are willing to make whatever changes are necessary to make their priorities clear. "I'm not going to let my work destroy my relationships at home."

I knew a precious couple who were going through a terrible time with one of their adult children. One of the parents said to me, "I look back on their childhood and think, 'what in the world did we do wrong?'" Because I knew how badly this parent was hurting, I didn't suggest any answers. But I couldn't help but flash back to a brief conversation I had with this child many years before. I asked, "How are you doing?"

The teen responded sullenly, "I guess I'm okay."

"So, where are your parents?"

"I never know anymore."

These parents had, I'm sure, told the teen where they would be. They were busy trying to do what needed to be done to maintain a beautiful home in a great neighborhood. They had to pay for private school and all the other activities that were so important to that child, *they thought*. That child would have traded all those things for more time with Mom and Dad.

Are you willing to pay the costly price of climate control? Are you going to take the time to determine the climate in your home? Have you decided to make the continued effort to clean out the worldly influences creeping into your home everyday? You're responsible for paying the high price in order to control the climate in your home.

You decide how people will talk in your home. If you don't want your kids to use foul language in your home, don't let the television, radio or stereo bring a bunch of foul language in. We no longer have television because of my tendency to let it become an addiction. Back when we had T.V., our teenage sons noticed that all the bad scenes and bad language during the shows they were watching occurred right as their parents walked into the room. The boys thought of it as an uncanny event, but we knew it was likely that they were simply more sensitized to what was on the screen when we were in the room. And, we were not reluctant to turn the television off.

Now that our boys are not at home, we are less sensitized to what we're watching, and this is a problem that must be dealt with as well. We find it much easier to use the off switch when our boys are around, so we've decided one solution to this problem is not to use the on switch. We can predict quite accurately what we'll be watching if we decide to turn the TV on, and it doesn't often fit with "whatever is true, whatever is noble, whatever is right, whatever is pure, whatever is lovely, whatever is admirable — if anything is excellent or praiseworthy — think about such things."[23]

Remember, if you have children and teens, they need their parents to be with them. We have used the words **appropriate** and **inappropriate** a lot with our boys. And, they knew we weren't going to have inappropriate stuff in our home. There were times when our boys didn't appreciate this, but they are appreciating it more and more now.

We are extremely pleased that our boys and their friends enjoyed hanging out at our house throughout their adolescence. In fact, many of their friends routinely drove several hours to spend their free time and holidays with us. Children learn to love parental climate-control, but you must do what it takes to control the climate. You have this authority, and God has given you this responsibility!

Dads, in particular, have authority in this regard. Dad should not leave it up to Mom to determine the parameters for the children. Dad needs to take his responsibility seriously, and Mom needs to encourage her husband's leadership, supporting him one hundred percent. Don't undermine each other's authority with the kids. Your children will appreciate the emotional security of parents who are united in their authority. Children want to know where the boundaries are. The more unified you are as parents, the more secure the boundaries, and the more secure your children will be all their lives.

Climate control involves many aspects of family life. It is vital to a healthy marriage. For instance, your bedroom should not be an office. Things more important than work are supposed to be happening in your bedroom. The climate in your bedroom should be one of romance, privacy, intimacy and celebration. Read *Song of Solomon*.

Children can ruin the climate-control in your bedroom? This is why you need to control their access to the bedroom. It's okay to nurse the infant in your room, but then they need to go back to their own room. Cultivate a protected atmosphere of intimacy and romance.

Don't blame the world **out there** for what's going on in your home. You are responsible. Society is really rotten, but do you know why? It's because the salt has lost its savor! It's not the pagans' fault that our country has become so decadent; church-going professing Christians have conformed to the world in conduct and expectations. Instead of being salty salt and shining lights, we've just tried to "fit in." We don't want to seem weird, and then we wonder, "Why are our homes falling apart?"

Climate control is costly, but it is essential. You are responsible. It takes energy to control the climate. If you don't use climate-control, houses and households quickly deteriorate. Houses will be reclaimed by nature and families will be reclaimed by the world, unless energy is expended for climate-control.

Remember, you belong to the Lord. Your home belongs to the Lord. You will give an account for the manner in which you invest your time and energy in building and maintaining a home that reflects God's glory.

Therefore, each of you must put off falsehood and speak truthfully to his neighbor, for we are all members of one body. ' In your anger do not sin': Do not let the sun go down while you are still angry, and do not give the devil a foothold. He who has been stealing must steal no longer, but must work, doing something useful with his own hands that he may have something to share with those in need.

Do not let any unwholesome talk come out of your mouths, but only what is helpful for building others up according to their needs, that it may benefit those who listen. And, do not grieve the Holy Spirit of God, with whom you were sealed for the day of redemption. Get rid of all bitterness, rage and anger, brawling and slander, along with every form of malice. Be kind and compassionate to one another, forgiving each other, just as in Christ God forgave you. . . .

From Ephesians 4:25 – 5:21.

Maintenance and Pest Control

IN EPHESIANS the apostle Paul gives us instructions about home life. No matter how well you build, maintenance is necessary. Certain things will be brought in that don't belong. So, we must routinely clean out both dirt and clutter.

In I Corinthians 6:12, the apostle Paul reminds us: "All things are lawful, but not all things are beneficial. All things are permissible, but not everything is helpful." Some things need to be cleaned out in order to make the atmosphere in the home more conducive to spiritual growth and development.

When our boys were elementary age, our family went for three years without television – not because real Christians don't watch T.V. Television is not the problem. Rather, the decision was based on the prayerful question, "What is best for our marriage and family at this time in our lives?" The good is often the enemy of the best. There are often things that aren't bad; they're just not as good as something that's better.

Much of what comes into the home is "tracked in" unintentionally. It comes in on the bottoms of your shoes or rides in on your coat. If we don't consciously, deliberately, routinely clean out what doesn't belong, our house will be a mess. Little by little, things that don't belong creep into our schedules, desires, ambitions, priorities, and budget. If you will look at the things coming into your home with conscientious discernment and decide to get rid of the things that aren't helpful, the quality of the atmosphere in your home will be greatly improved.

AFTER WE'D BEEN LIVING in the mountains for several years, my wife found a rattlesnake in our garage and was rather upset about it. So, I killed the rattlesnake. But a week later, there was another rattlesnake in the garage. This told me it was time to clean out the garage. We didn't have a bunch of *bad* stuff in the garage, just a bunch of stuff we didn't need. It gave the snakes a place to hide. It also gave the mice a place to hide, which was why the snakes were hanging out there. When you get rid of the stuff that doesn't belong, all of a sudden the critters that don't belong go away too.

Paul says, "Get rid of all bitterness, rage and anger, brawling and slander, along with every form of malice. Be kind and compassionate to one another, forgiving each other, just as in Christ God forgave you."[24] So many problems would be solved if people would learn how to forgive. No one will ever be able to earn forgiveness. If it has to be earned, it's not forgiveness.

Even after you have forgiven those who have wronged you and sought forgiveness from those you have wronged, you must guard your heart. You must protect areas that are exposed, so the environment outside won't penetrate and destroy what you have built – the greater the exposure to the outside elements, the greater the need for protection.

Think about this from the standpoint of your physical house. You don't paint the inside of the board where there is no exposure to the elements; you paint the outside parts that are exposed to the weather. Why do you apply paint, stain or sealer on the outside of your house? You want it to last, so you put the paint on to keep the sun and water from destroying the wood.

But, what happens after you paint a house? Eventually, paint peels and chips, and you have to come back and paint again. To do it right, you have to prepare the surface before you paint. The most challenging part of painting is all the prep work to get it ready. You have to clean the dirt off to get the surface prepped. If you don't clean away the stuff that doesn't belong, the paint won't stick. It might look good temporarily, but after a short time, it will begin flaking and peeling.

We must find the areas in our lives needing special protection. Because we can't separate from this sinful world, we tend to compartmentalize our lives. Ironically, many people use almost no protection for the parts of their lives that are out in the world, because they want to blend in. Then, they come to church with barriers in place, trying to appear holy. Yet, the place where we need to be protected, where we need buffers and insulation, is out in the world.

Church is where we're supposed to be able to come for help and healing. We need to be able to come and be vulnerable with our brothers and sisters in Christ. We should be transparently honest, requesting prayer and help. Instead, we come into church and put up barriers of protection in order to appear holy and in control. We go back out into the world and "get real." This is backwards. When we start rotting, we wonder what's wrong. So, we just put up barriers again back in church, "Praise God. My family's fine. How about yours? I bet you're fine too." We are insulated and protected at church and exposed to the world.

I'm not suggesting we should be phony out in the world. I'm suggesting we need to be conscious of the fact that we mustn't let the world squeeze us into its mold. Romans 12 says, "Don't be conformed to the pattern of this world."

What does this mean if we're talking about siding on your house? It means that when it's wet outside, you want the wood to still be dry. You don't let the atmosphere outside penetrate and determine the composition inside.

In practical terms, I will continually communicate with my heavenly Father in prayer, and I will saturate my mind with scripture. When I'm bombarded with the world's lies, I will refuse to embrace them.

I HEARD A STORY about two guys out walking their dogs. One had a Doberman and the other had a Chihuahua. They were walking down the sidewalk together, and one said to the other, "I'm hungry."

The other said, "Me too."

"It sure would be nice if we could stop down here at the restaurant on the corner and get something good to eat."

"They'd never let us in with our pets."

"Why don't we just tell them they're seeing eye dogs?"

The guy with the Chihuahua said, "I don't think they'd buy that."

The guy with the Doberman replied, "With the Americans with Disabilities Act, I think we can intimidate them. Let's give it a try."

"You go first."

They put on their sunglasses, and the guy with the Doberman went in and said, "I'd like a table please."

The waiter said, "I'm sorry sir. I can't let you in with the pet."

He responded, "This is a guide dog."

The waiter asked incredulously, "A Doberman is a guide dog?"

"Yes, they're using Dobermans more and more now as guide dogs. They make great Seeing Eye dogs."

The waiter reluctantly seated him.

The guy with the Chihuahua walked in and said, "Excuse me, I'd like a table please."

The waiter said, "I'm sorry sir, but I can't allow your pet in here."

"This is my Seeing Eye dog."

"Sir, you're trying to tell me a Chihuahua is a Seeing Eye dog."

The man excitedly exclaimed, *"A Chihuahua? They gave me a Chihuahua?"*

I TOLD THIS STORY to the kids at the Ranch and after everyone had a good laugh, I asked them, "What's wrong with this story?"

They responded immediately, "It makes lying seem like a good thing."

We are teaching our students at the Ranch to think critically. On the one hand, this is a funny joke, but not because lying is funny. It's funny because of the element of surprise. The irony catches you off guard. While we can tell our students such a joke, we are also teaching them how to think so they don't just laugh and subliminally accept the idea that if you can trick people, it's cute. It's not cute. It's wrong. Satan is a liar and the father of lies. If we try to deceive other people, we're not doing something funny, cute, or humorous.

If we want to keep from being saturated by the world's values, we have to erect barriers by learning how to think biblically as we apply the truths of Scripture to every situation. This is what it means in Romans 12:2 when we are told to continually have our minds renewed: "Do not conform any longer to the pattern of this world, but be transformed by the renewing of your mind. Then you will be able to test and approve what God's will is—his good, pleasing and perfect will."

Notice the pattern that Paul sets forth. First, he says, "Don't let the world squeeze you into its mold," or "don't be conformed to the pattern of this world." He then explains the alternative and the results, "Instead be transformed by the renewing of your mind so that you can demonstrate God's will for your life to be that which is good, acceptable, and perfect."

As we yield our lives to God in obedience, we resist the pressures of the world. As we have our minds renewed by scripture, our lives are transformed. This is routine maintenance. This is why the spiritual disciplines of prayer, Bible study, and fellowship become so important. This is how we stay clean. This is how we stay on track. This is why it's important to meet with fellow believers to study and discuss the Bible and important issues of our day. There are all kinds of wrong ideas bombarding our lives continually with messages about what will make us happy and what will make our marriages and family life good. We have to weigh these things in the light of the Bible and see if these messages are consistent with God's truth.

My wife and I have had some wonderful, happy vacations. We've gone to some nice resorts and enjoyed great food and fun. I would say, however, that of all the trips we've taken, the one that means the most to us was not a vacation. It was a trip to Ukraine in the former Soviet Union. We lived in the most impoverished and difficult surroundings we've ever been in.

Neither of us grew up in affluence, but we have always lived better than the people in the old Soviet Bloc. Even highly educated people who have achieved worldly success under the old Soviet system didn't live anywhere near as well as the lower middle class in America. Yet, even in these unpleasant surroundings, that trip meant the most to us.

The things the world offers don't bring real joy. If we'll seek first the kingdom of God and his righteousness, everything we need will be given to us

Don't be afraid to put God first and to do what he says. He offers a whole different kind of riches, riches that will satisfy for eternity.

Repairing and Replacing

We cannot act as if our home is going to maintain itself. We must be committed to repairing and replacing what breaks. From time to time things will break, regardless of the great foundation laid and the competent builder. Wear and tear will occur. In our relationships with each other, there will be times when we have to go back and repair a break. There will be times when we have to fix something that's wrong.

In the book, **When Two Become One,** I suggested couples should memorize four key phrases:

"I'm sorry. That was wrong of me. Please forgive me. I'm glad I'm married to you."

All four of these are essential. Use them to help repair your marriage relationship when you've helped precipitate a break. You don't have to be the only one at fault to be the one to initiate the repairs.

There will also be times when you have to replace something. I'm not talking about replacing your mate. There may be a tradition, habit, or something else that was once helpful in your marriage, but it's no longer needed. If it's not beneficial, it may be time to get rid of it; sometimes, hanging on to the wrong thing results in disaster. Replacement is a necessary part of life. Be prepared to replace old traditions, restaurants, vacation destinations, or whatever it is. It is important to be willing to invest the time, energy and cost in repairing and replacing when it becomes necessary. Do it! Don't just sit there and wish things were different. Pay the price and make the change.

Pest Control

Pest Control is a necessary part of routine maintenance. Remember that pests include things unseen as well as those that are visible. Most of the things that will destroy your home will not be obvious at the time.

Sometimes we see indoor pests like mice and roaches. We just got e-mail from a friend on a short-term missions trip to Costa Rica. As the group was eating around the kitchen table, their host suddenly took a dart and blowgun to shoot and kill rats running along the kitchen shelves. I am confident my friend lost weight on that trip, as I would have.

Nobody wants pests running around, but for most of us, it's the unseen pests that are much more likely to do damage. Rats have fleas and can do damage. Roaches carry germs. Years ago, I had a two-inch roach jump onto my bare chest in the middle of the night in

Texas. I wanted to scream as loudly as possible as I fought to knock the roach off my chest, but I didn't want to wake my hosts and the rest of the household. I made no sound except for the sounds of my hands beating on my chest as I batted the roach away.

There are times when you see the pests, but far more often, the pests that destroy our relationships are unseen. What's the worst thing about a roach? It's the germs on the roach. I'm much bigger than the roach or the germs, but germs can get inside, penetrate, and make a difference in our health. They'll make us sick. When we deal with pest control, we need to remember to watch out for the unseen things.

In order for termites to survive, they have to stay hidden, and not just because we would kill them. They can't be out where the air is dry. They've got to have moisture. As long as they have moisture, they can eat sheetrock, wood, phone books, and every kind of cellulose. They have a wonderful time chewing up everything that makes our houses stand. If they are forced out into the air, they will dry out and die. When you see tunnels on the outside of block or stone, termites are inside. It's time to get help or lose the house.

Get rid of the pests and put up barriers so they can't get back in. Replace what they have destroyed. You may find where bitterness, greed, selfishness, and thoughtlessness have brought damage into your home and your relationships. Get rid of sin and unforgiveness and repair what's been damaged. Realize it's not just the obvious problems. Sometimes you have to uncover areas to see what's really going on.

Three important principles

Seek to seal off as many means of entry as possible.

Look to see where the things, which don't belong in your home or in your life, are getting in.

We had what sounded like a squirrel in the attic. It turned out to be mice. They just sound very big when they are running around overhead. We couldn't just get rid of those mice, we had to find out where they were getting in and block the way as best we could. They'll still find other ways in, but there won't be as many. Seal off as many ways as possible. Don't ever just leave the doors open in your home.

Do you understand the application? Put screens on the windows if you want to keep the birds and bats out. Gnats may get in through the screen, but it beats chasing a bird around. Please, consider the application with television. And, I want to warn you that the parental controls on the Internet don't work. Teens are being targeted by pornographers. Children cannot surf the Internet safely without adult supervision. I'm not saying not to have an Internet connection; I'm warning you that you can't make the Internet safe for unsupervised children. And, many adults are susceptible to these *pests*, too.

Show zero tolerance for pests that get inside.

How many mice are too many to have in your house? Mice multiply exponentially. Start early to eliminate the pests. Don't wait for the infestation. God's standard of holiness is perfection. The agricultural department has a different standard. They actually publish standards outlining the percentage of rat feces, insect parts, and other undesirable items, which is considered acceptable in foods for consumers. It's such an endemic problem that a standard has been established.

We live in a fallen world and we're going to be ingesting stuff we don't want to know about. To a certain extent, we live a symbiotic relationship with pests. But, when you have visible evidence of pests, you need to take action immediately. Have a zero tolerance approach. You don't have to go out and destroy all termites in the world, but show zero tolerance for termites in your house.

Show zero tolerance for greed, bitterness, malice, sexual impurity, lying and all forms of deceit: "Among you there must not be even a hint of sexual immorality or any kind of impurity or of greed."[25] You have the authority and responsibility to show zero tolerance for pests in your home.

Praise is a remarkable and wonderful barrier of protection around your home. It's amazing how God can use praise to bless and protect your family and to minister to other people as well.

Try to get rid of the places where pests hide and the things they like to eat.

If there are things in your life that feed greed, bitterness or lust, get rid of that stuff. It doesn't belong. It's not just the bad stuff that needs to go. It's the clutter, too — anything that provides a place for Satan to slip in and do his work.

Proper maintenance and pest control make for the kind of homes that will stand when storms come. This is what God wants for us. My wife and I have been married twenty-five years, and I can honestly tell you it's getting better every year. I'm in love with her and she's in love with me. I'm so grateful God's plan for us is not simply survival. God's plan is that we would be more than conquerors through him who loved us. God's plan is good, acceptable and perfect! Don't miss it!

ENDNOTES

[1] Matthew 7:24,25.

[2] Job 3:25

[3] Job 1:13-25.

[4] Job 2:6-13.

[5] Job 3:25

[6] I Thessalonians 4:13

[7] Matthew 28:20

[8] II Corinthians 12:7-10.

[9] James 1:2,3; I Peter 1:3-9; I Peter 4:12,13.

[10] I Corinthians 15:19

[11] John 16:33

[12] Philippians 4:11-13.

[13] Kyle Matthews, ©1993 BMG Songs, Inc./Above the Rim Music, ASCAP. Used with permission.

[14] John 11:43

[15] John 15:7

[16] Acts 16:25-26

[17] Philippians 4:7

[18] John 16:33

[19] Philippians 3:10

[20] John 10:18

[21] John 15:1-8

[22] Luke 11:39

[23] Philippians 4:8

[24] Ephesians 4:31

[25] Ephesians 5:3

INFORMATION
JIM WOOD MINISTRIES
P.O. Box 1600
Pigeon Forge, TN 37868
Jwood@wvr.org

❖ To schedule preaching, seminars or retreats
❖ To order more copies of this book
❖ For other books or audio tapes
Order on-line @ www.wvr.org
Or 865/429-4300

Also available: A FOUR VOLUME VIDEO SERIES
A Place to Call Home — issues concerning you and your family,
hosted by Jim and Susan Wood
Topics include:
Forgiveness and Trust
Discipline
Overcoming a Spirit of Fear
Help for single parents
Teaching your child about sex
Finding your identity in Christ

WEARS VALLEY RANCH **www.wvr.org**
volunteer missions opportunities at WVR 865/429-5437

WVR is operated through the generosity of our donors.
Contributions to JIM WOOD MINISTRIES enable us to print and
distribute books, videos and audiotapes, all available for a suggested
donation. Thank you!